# Andy P

## *red mo*

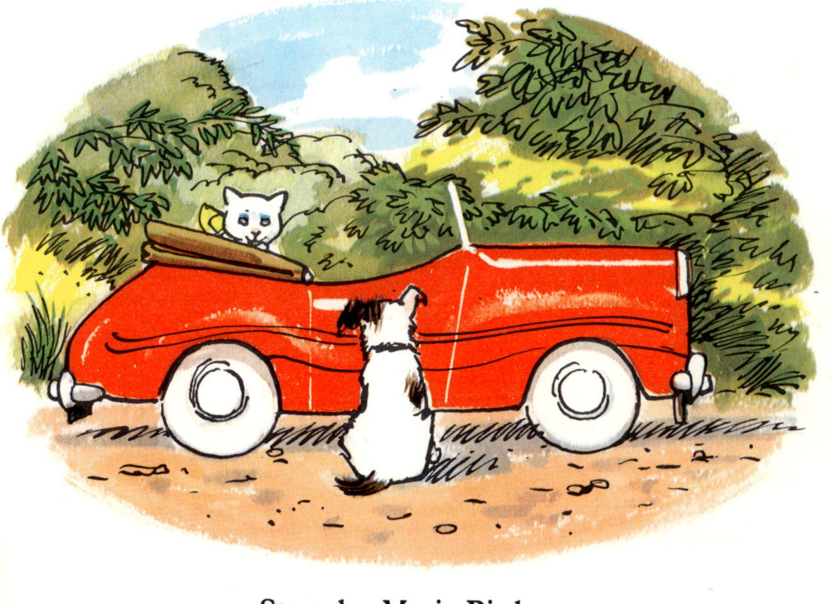

Story by Maria Bird

Illustrated by Matvyn Wright

HODDER AND STOUGHTON

Andy Pandy has a little white kitten and a puppy called Rags, and they and he and Teddy all live in Andy Pandy's house with a friend called Looby Loo. She is a very clever rag doll.

One day when Andy and Teddy were busy cleaning Andy's red motor car, the white kitten got tired of watching, and wandered off by himself. Rags didn't go because he was digging up a bone.

Afterwards Looby Loo went indoors and tidied the house. Andy Pandy and Teddy often leave their toys lying about, and only that morning Teddy had trodden in the kitten's milk and just left it there on the floor.

The sun was shining and the white kitten pranced along until he came to a pond, and he thought, 'Why can't I have fish for dinner? A whole fish all to myself, and not just bits and pieces?'

When Andy Pandy and Teddy had finished the car it looked like new.
'Now it wants to go out,' Teddy said. 'Let's go for a picnic after dinner.'
Rags didn't want any dinner, because he had found his bone, and the white kitten wasn't there.

AP 123

He had climbed a tree and was walking along a branch hanging over the pond. Looking down he could see little fishes swimming about, and his eyes turned as green as grass, which they do when he's naughty.

He crept carefully along until he saw a big stone in the middle of the pond. Then he sprang off the branch on to the stone. But he soon found it wasn't easy to catch fishes with paws, and he grew very cross.

To make things worse, the sun went in and it began to rain. He couldn't reach the branch. He was cold and wet and frightened, and he began to cry. Miaow! Miaow! No one heard him.

But someone saw him. Looby Loo was looking out of the window, and far away she could just see the kitten in the middle of the pond. Rags had come in because of the rain. The clean red motor car stood outside getting wet.

'Look,' said Looby. 'Tell Andy that the white kitten is in danger.' Rags dropped his bone and rushed into the kitchen, barking and pulling at Andy's rompers. 'Something's happened,' Andy cried. 'Come on, Teddy, we'll follow Rags.'

They jumped into the red motor car and pedalled after Rags, who took them to the pond, where they saw the white kitten shivering and crying on the big stone. 'I'll go in and get her,' said brave little Teddy.

AP 123

'No,' said Andy, 'I'll go.' But Rags was already jumping into the water and swimming towards the kitten. 'Go back and fetch some towels, Teddy,' said Andy. Teddy felt very proud to be driving the car alone, and he pedalled as fast as his little fat legs would go.

AP 123

When Teddy came back with the towels, Rags, very tired, had almost reached the bank with the white kitten in his mouth. Andy Pandy pulled them both out, and they were soon wrapped in dry towels.

Then they all went home, and while Andy Pandy and Teddy went up to dry themselves, Looby Loo dried Rags and the white kitten. 'Don't you ever run away again,' she said. 'No, I won't,' said the white kitten, and his eyes were as blue as forget-me-nots.

When everyone was dry Teddy said, ‘We won’t get our picnic now. Just look at the car, all splashed with mud.’ ‘That doesn’t matter,’ Andy said. ‘We’ve got our kitten and the very bravest dog that ever was.’

AP 123

## ANDY PANDY BOOKS

Andy Pandy and the Green Puppy
Andy Pandy and the Badger
Andy Pandy and the Patchwork Cat
Andy Pandy's Little Goat
Andy Pandy and the Scarecrow
Andy Pandy's Dovecot
Andy Pandy and the Teddy Dog
Andy Pandy's Washing Day
Andy Pandy and the Hedgehog
Andy Pandy Paints His House
Andy Pandy and the White Kitten
Andy Pandy's Jack-in-the-box
Andy Pandy's New Pet
Andy Pandy in the Country
Andy Pandy's Weather House
Andy Pandy's Shop
Andy Pandy's Red Motor Car
Andy Pandy and the Willow Tree
Andy Pandy and the Gingerbread Man
Andy Pandy and the Snowman
Andy Pandy's Playhouse
Andy Pandy and the Spotted Cow
Andy Pandy and the Yellow Dog
Andy Pandy's Puppy
Andy Pandy's Baby Pigs